In the Spirit of a Dream

THIRTEEN STORIES OF AMERICAN IMMIGRANTS OF COLOR

DEVELOPED BY **ALINA CHAU**

WRITTEN BY **AIDA SALAZAR**

ILLUSTRATED BY

ALINA CHAU | BIANCA DIAZ | DION MBD | FAHMIDA AZIM

GABY D'ALESSANDRO | JOSE RAMIREZ | KEN DALEY | NICOLE XU

PAULO D. CAMPOS | RAHELE JOMEPOUR BELL | TRACY GUITEAU

VANESSA FLORES | YAS IMAMURA

In the Spirit of Spirit of a Dream

SCHOLASTIC PRESS | NEW YORK

Text copyright © 2021 by Aida Salazar | Illustrations copyright © 2021 by Alina Chau, Bianca Diaz, Dion MBD, Fahmida Azim, Gaby D'Alessandro, Jose Ramirez, Ken Daley, Nicole Xu, Paulo D. Campos, Paul Davey, Rahele Jomepour Bell, Tracy Guiteau, Vanessa Flores, Yas Imamura | Published by Scholastic Press, an imprint of Scholastic Inc., *Publishers since 1920.* SCHOLASTIC, SCHOLASTIC PRESS, and associated logos are trademarks and/or registered trademarks of Scholastic Inc. | The publisher does not have any control over and does not assume any responsibility for author or third-party websites or their content. | No part of this publication may be reproduced, stored in a retrieval system, or transmitted in any form or by any means, electronic, mechanical, photocopying, recording, or otherwise, without written permission of the publisher. For information regarding permission, write to Scholastic Inc., Attention: Permissions Department, 557 Broadway, New York, NY 10012. | Library of Congress Cataloging-in-Publication Data Available
ISBN 978-1-338-55287-4 | 10 9 8 7 6 5 4 3 2 1 | 21 22 23 24 25 | Printed in China 38 | First edition, November 2021

To my friends and professors at the UCLA Animation Workshop who made America my home. — A. C.

For my parents, Maria Isabel Salazar Viramontes and Fidel Rafael Salazar. Thank you for dreaming. — A. S.

In the Spirit of a Dream

ILLUSTRATED BY ALINA CHAU

We set out across
   continents,
   oceans,
   and borders,
to find a place where we have been told
our dreams can be made — the United States of America.

We come
as migrants, often unwanted,
to this country that will always belong
to the first nations to inhabit it,
was built largely by
those enslaved and forced here,
together with those
who are immigrants, like us.

We follow a dream
that doesn't always come true.
Sometimes, it fades before us
yet we persist and pursue it
to awaken a future of our own.

These are some of our stories,
the songs of our spirits,
our longings,
the challenges, and the heights
to which we have risen
in search of fulfilling
our wildest imaginations.

Alejandro Albor *PARALYMPIC HANDCYCLIST*

ILLUSTRATED BY BIANCA DIAZ

At fifteen, Alejandro came
to the United States from Mexico
with his family, to labor as farmworkers.
    A dreamer driven to fit in, to learn English,
    to rise, and be a pro boxer one day.

Not soon after, his bright life
was nearly extinguished
when the car he was driving
collided with an oncoming train.

He survived the wreckage
without the use of both his legs.

As his body healed,
    the sun of hope began to shine
    illuminating new ideas and abilities.

Alejandro propelled himself into handcycling.

With each pedal and stroke of his three-wheeled machine
    moved by the strength of his arms
    and the determination to do something great,
he became a Paralympic athlete.

The skill and radiance of his racing
pushed hard against any wind
leading him to win two Olympic Medals for the US —
    ultimate symbols of a dream.

Anousheh Ansari *ASTRONAUT*

ILLUSTRATED BY RAHELE JOMEPOUR BELL

With her little feet planted on Iranian soil,
Anousheh wished to be an astronaut,
    to fly into space and soar among the stars.
But the Iranian Revolution came
and the horrors of that war
tried to wipe those dreams away
    until she came to the United States.
Here the many languages that
    surrounded her flew into her ears
    and stayed — English, French, and Russian.
She never forgot the beloved Persian sounds
of her birthplace.
    The languages of math, science, engineering
    became her strength,
her ticket to become
the first female private space explorer
and the first astronaut of Iranian descent
    to float among the stars.

Ayub Khan Ommaya *SURGEON AND INVENTOR*

ILLUSTRATED BY NICOLE XU

A renaissance coursed through Ayub's veins
    a limitless bounty of what he could do.
He excelled with bravado
    as he swam into a national championship,
boxed with skill for rounds in the ring,
    and rowed for miles along a river.
He invented things that only an imagination so free could bring
    like an airbag helmet to help protect people when they fall.
He sang operas with gusto before performing surgeries,
    a musical rush helping him save countless lives,
    like those of the man
from whose head he pulled a tendril-like tumor
in an operation lasting nineteen hours.

Ayub and his light came from Pakistan.
He made history in the United States and beyond
    with his inventive dreams,
    his unstoppable courage,
    and his love of life.

Cándido Camero *PERCUSSIONIST*

ILLUSTRATED BY KEN DALEY

Cándido was a virtuoso percussionist
when he left Cuba for New York City in the 1940s
with nothing but the dream
    to share the magic of his music
    with the world.

A conga drummer whose Afro-Cuban blood
lined the perfect rhythms that he played,
Cándido was one of the first
    to bring these sounds to jazz.

Cándido's dream rose like an incantation,
he played with the most famous
jazz orchestras around the country.
His drum, drum, drumming
    popped out of crackly radio speakers,
    clubs, and dance halls alike.

He spellbound with his innovation
    played three congas when others played one,
    added a guiro and bell when others never imagined,
    he tuned his conga drums to play a melody
    to create a sweet and rhythmic tune.

But he endured segregation and racism
because he was Black in his new country.
He often had to sleep on the tour bus
because whites-only hotels didn't allow him to stay,
or enter through back doors of whites-only clubs
where he was the featured performer.

Cándido, a pioneer of jazz and the Afro-Cuban mambo,
Cándido, whose love of the drum
    and wish to spread the joy of his music
    drove him to persist.

Conceição Damasceno *CHOREOGRAPHER*

ILLUSTRATED BY PAULO D. CAMPOS

A chrysalis lived in Conceição's heart
that nested a dream
　　to dance
　　　　to flutter
　　　　　　and glide above
the Brazilian bahia
where she was born.
　　　　The movement of samba,
　　　　　　the whirl of Orixás,
　　　　　　the blessings of her mother,
　　　　　　　　the Amazon filling her lungs,
　　　　　　　　　　opening and lifting her wings,
　　　　defining the beauty of her sway.

She soared
　　a borboleta
　　　　a butterfly in all its grace,
beyond the dirt floors that raised her,
beyond the dance schools that trained her.
　　　　She came to land in another bay, in the United States.

Here the swell of all that made her
spun to full splendor with
　　　　BrasArte, her very own dance studio and dance company,
　　　　the numerous shows she choreographed and directed,
　　　　the countless San Francisco Carnavals in which she paraded,
　　　　the many showcases to help other immigrant artists,
　　　　the beautiful Brazilian Day & Lavagem Festival
　　　　　　she launched in the streets.

She infuses each of her creations with the spirit of Brazil
and makes all those who experience them
feel the joy and elegance of her dream in flight.

David Tran *ENTREPRENEUR*

I L L U S T R A T E D   B Y   A L I N A   C H A U

David dreamed things
would be better in the United States,
that he could leave the war in Vietnam behind
and find a new life
    brimming with possibility,
that he could stir all of his hope
into a spicy sauce people would like.

David made his first batch in Vietnam
    and called it Pepper Sa-te.
He put it in recycled baby jars and sold it
while pedaling his bike through
the war-torn streets of his neighborhood.
    He so believed in his tasty sauce.

This dream sailed across the sea
with him when he escaped Vietnam
    on a ship called *Huy Fong*.
Huy Fong, the perfect name
for his new company, in his new home.
    David's dream was on its way.

Encouraged by the smiling faces of his customers
and his family, who cheered and helped him, too,
he continued to stir and mix until
    his most delicious
    most spicy
    most secret
    and ooh aahing sauce
    was ready.

David named this one, Sriracha!

Everyone raved about Sriracha's yumminess
as word moved from happy mouth to happy mouth.
Now the world over enjoys the recipe
    of a man who dared to stir hope into a sauce.

Dikembe Mutombo
HUMANITARIAN AND BASKETBALL PLAYER

ILLUSTRATED BY DION MBD

When Dikembe came to study
at Georgetown University in the United States,
   he dreamed of becoming a doctor,
   to speak to his patients
   in the nine languages he would learn,
to make his family of educators
and those in his community
in the Democratic Republic of the Congo proud.

He stood taller than anyone on campus
and was soon recruited
   to play basketball for the first time.

His newfound talent flourished on the court.
   Swoosh. Block. Pass. Block again.
He did things he never imagined.
   Unleashing his fierce shot-blocking power
from college to many teams in the NBA,
   Dikembe rose to become a four-time
NBA Defensive Player of the Year
and an eight-time All-Star.
   Swoosh!

Fans cheered for the Congolese man
with a heart of gold who never forgot
the root of the one dream
he held close —
   to lift people with medicine.

When he retired from the NBA
he built a modern medical facility back home.
   He and his talents
   the pride of the Congo.

Edwidge Danticat *AUTHOR*

ILLUSTRATED BY TRACY GUITEAU

Stories slid into Edwidge's curious mind
when as a child, she listened to her elders
retell their lives and myths in the midst
of blackouts on her island home of Haiti,
    a home she would leave for the US
      when she was twelve years old.

As she grew in Brooklyn,
the shape of her life was sculpted
by new city streets that moved her,
by what she remembered,
by the will to read, to write,
to dream, to call into being
    her own stories, whispered by ancestors,
    and an abundant imagination.

What sprung forth was a lineage of books —
one after the next, awarded for excellence —
with stories of Haitians, immigrants,
women, brothers, and families
    who collect their pains and their loves
    and offer them in the palms of their warm hands.

The stories Edwidge tells resound,
Krik? Krak! a Haitian call and response,
    carried into fullness by her immigrant pen
    and the breath of the island.

Ilhan Omar *REPRESENTATIVE TO CONGRESS*

ILLUSTRATED BY FAHMIDA AZIM

Ilhan began to understand injustice
when the war in Somalia sent her away from home,
forced her and her family into a Kenyan refugee camp.
    The dream for shelter and safety,
    a distant garden of longing.

They came to the US
to plant new seeds, asylum granted.
Here Ilhan began
to turn what was thought of her
    as girl
    as Muslim
    as refugee
into a bouquet for others,
into a heart that mattered,
into a voice that could speak against injustice,
to try to undo its terrible grip on those who suffer.

Her light and knowing bloomed
in the service of each community she touched
    as citizen
    as educator
    as organizer
    as legislator
responding with grace and dignity
when faced with violence and hate.
Her gifts grew so full she was elected
    to the United States House of Representatives,
    the first Somali American refugee
    to be elected to the House,
    and the first woman of color
    to serve as a US representative from Minnesota.

Her garden of justice flowering.

Jim Lee *COMIC BOOK ARTIST*

ILLUSTRATED BY VANESSA FLORES

The language of comics
is one Jim first learned
when he came to the US as a boy
and only spoke Korean.

Jim boomed into drawing
searching to bring to life
his sense of being an outsider
like the superheroes he drew.

Through long days at his drafting table
sketching and repeating
a superpower of his own emerged.
His art made you *feel* the story
without words
through the movement of lines,
the richness of details,
the emotion in drawn faces.

Jim wielded his talent at Marvel Comics
crafting comic worlds
he'd studied and dreamed
ultimately penciling and co-writing
X-Men No. 1.

His storytelling
catapulted him to stardom
as this work remains
the highest-selling comic book
of all time.

Juana Gutiérrez *COMMUNITY ORGANIZER*

ILLUSTRATED BY JOSE RAMIREZ

Juana came from another terrain.
Yes, Mexico birthed her, but it was in
East Los Angeles, where her own children
were born, that the urgency to keep the earth
pristine and healthy became her mission.

When corporations and the government
wanted to destroy her neighborhood,
Juana led the charge.
She alerted her neighbors.
She organized at her church.
She talked to anyone who would listen
and formed Madres del Este de Los Angeles, Santa Isabel (MELASI).

NO! she yelled alongside outraged mothers.
NOT IN OUR BACKYARD!
NO! to the government that wanted to build a prison
where their children played.
NO! to the toxic waste dump that would poison their air and water.
NO! to the oil pipeline that would rip through their neighborhoods.

Juana knew
though they were poor and immigrant
they deserved clean earth
like everyone else.

Many doors closed, many tears fell,
but they didn't give up
and won each time!

Juana's and MELASI's work inspired people
in other countries struggling for the same.
People saw their dreams for their children,
their love of the earth,
their strength
to make a change.

Yo-Yo Ma *CELLIST*

ILLUSTRATED BY GABY D'ALESSANDRO

Yo-Yo Ma was born
 into a cradle of music.
A Chinese boy living in France
nourished by his father's rich musical teachings,
he fell in love
 with the cello
 when he was only four.
The round sound of music
made his bow dance with splendor.

In the US, his stunning ability
would make him
a world-class cellist,
 the most famous
 modern classical musician.

With his music as a source of connection,
he traveled across the globe
 and a new dream emerged,
to not only play beautiful music
 but to live beautifully, too.

To use his art to experience
the music of other countries
 and play his songs of wonder
 for new audiences.
For the music
 to be of service to others
 to search for the places
where music transcends differences,
 heals, and touches
 others with heart.

Yo-Yo Ma *CELLIST*

Undocupoets *POETS*

ILLUSTRATED BY YAS IMAMURA

Poems fell from their pens
onto pages after pages
 about a sweetheart,
 or sailing on a cloud,
 or the bonds of family.
Poems about living in the shadows,
 for being undocumented,
 and immigrant to this land.

Marcelo, Javier, Christopher
came together to form
the Undocupoets,
 with poems after poems
 ready for publishing
 and worthy for contests to consider.

But their work had no place
within the many poetry award contests
 that said: YOU MUST BE A CITIZEN.
Their citizen-less words dashed
from the dream of being published
 into a tight quiet knot of silence.

Until they wrote an open letter
asking for this rule to be changed.

Their letter succeeded and became a movement.
With Janine and Esther they grew
into an organization.

Now the Undocupoets help others,
 documented or not,
 place their poems in
 the pages of books
 for all to read.

Immigrant Parents

ILLUSTRATED BY ALINA CHAU

In the spirit of a dream
we build what we can.
We are not always successful.
    We stumble.
        Often, we fall
on roads not
    as friendly or sure
as we imagined,
but the spirit persists.

What we receive is a gift
a path paved for our children
who carry our yearnings
inside themselves, too.
    Gentle and bright
        as a nautical star,
guiding their own journey
        toward different dreams.
Grounded in humility
grown from our risks,
        our labor
        our hope
        our love.

Alejandro Albor

I L L U S T R A T E D   B Y BIANCA DIAZ

Alejandro Albor is a handcyclist born in Michoacán, Mexico. When he was fifteen years old, he and his family relocated to the United States. He lost the use of his legs below the knee at the age of eighteen, in a car accident with a moving train. He dreamed of being an Olympic boxer. After the accident, he continued to pursue his love of athletics and excelled in a different sport — handcycling. Meanwhile, he earned a college degree in airframe and power plants and worked for the Army Corps of Engineers. After four years of cycling training, Alejandro won two silver medals and one bronze medal at the 2004 and 2008 Paralympic Games. He is also a five-time winner of the world's longest wheelchair and handcycle race, the Sadler's Ultra Challenge; and he has won multiple marathons, including the Miami Marathon. Albor is also a business owner and runs A-WON HandCycles.

Anousheh Ansari

I L L U S T R A T E D   B Y RAHELE JOMEPOUR BELL

Anousheh Ansari is an engineer, space tourist, and CEO. Born in Mashhad, Iran, Anousheh lived through the Iranian Revolution and immigrated as a teenager to the United States in 1984. She always dreamed of being an astronaut, which drew her to study science, engineering, and multiple languages. On September 18, 2006, a few days after her fortieth birthday, Anousheh earned a place in history as the first female private space explorer, the fourth private explorer, and the first astronaut of Iranian descent to visit space. She has received multiple awards for her entrepreneurial excellence. She is the CEO of the XPRIZE Foundation, whose mission is to award prizes to those who best "bring about radical breakthroughs for the benefit of humanity."

Ayub Khan Ommaya

I L L U S T R A T E D   B Y NICOLE XU

Dr. Ayub Khan Ommaya was a Muslim French Pakistani American neurosurgeon, inventor, and leading expert in traumatic brain injuries. He was a national champion swimmer, and during medical school at Oxford University, an amateur boxer and member of the college crew team. He was also a trained opera tenor who often sang before and after surgery. Ayub came to the United States in 1961 as a visiting scientist, and later became an associate neurosurgeon. He was part of a team of surgeons who saved the life of a teacher, removing a rare growth of life-threatening blood vessels at the base of his brain over the course of a nineteen-hour operation. Ayub invented an inflatable collar, similar to an airbag, that attaches to motorcycle helmets to protect against spinal injury. Another of Ayub's inventions, the Ommaya reservoir, is an implant that helps sufferers of brain tumors and hydrocephalus. This invention coincidentally saved the life of Aida Salazar's immigrant father.

Cándido Camero

ILLUSTRATED BY KEN DALEY

Afro-Cuban conga virtuoso Cándido Camero is credited with being one of the first percussionists to bring conga drumming to jazz and to help in the development of the mambo and Afro-Cuban jazz. Born in Havana, Cuba, in 1921, he came to the United States in 1946 and got his start by playing with jazz pianist Billy Taylor. By the 1950s, Cándido was a featured soloist with the Stan Kenton Orchestra, with whom he toured the United States. He became one of the best known congueros in the country, appearing on popular television shows of the time. He recorded and performed with many in the field of jazz, including such luminaries as Miles Davis, Dizzy Gillespie, and Charlie Parker. He was named a "legend of jazz" and was the subject of the 2006 documentary *Cándido: Hands of Fire*. Cándido died on November 7, 2020, at age 99.

Conceição Damasceno

ILLUSTRATED BY PAULO D. CAMPOS

Dancer, choreographer, instructor, and artistic director Conceição Damasceno was born in Bahia, Brazil, and is known for her signature dance technique. From an early age, she studied and did extensive research in Afro-Brazilian folklore and religion. She has performed throughout Brazil, the United States, Europe, and Asia, opening for major artists, including Gilberto Gil, Margareth Menezes, Celia Cruz, and Tito Puente. Conceição has represented Brazilian culture for nearly thirty years in San Francisco's annual Carnaval Parade and in the founding of BrasArte, a Brazilian cultural organization in Berkeley. She has staged critically acclaimed dance theater productions. Most notably, she founded the annual Brazilian Day & Lavagem Festival — the largest festival of its kind in the San Francisco Bay Area.

David Tran

ILLUSTRATED BY ALINA CHAU

David Tran served as a major in the army of South Vietnam. In 1979, he fled communist Vietnam on a freighter from Soc Trang to the United States, along with 3,317 people. He went on to found a sauce company in Los Angeles, Huy Fong Foods, which he named after the Taiwanese freighter that carried him to safety. David produced his first hot sauce, called Pepper Sa-te, in 1975, while he was still in Vietnam. When in the US, David invented one of the most famous hot sauces in the entire world — Sriracha. The rooster symbol comes from the fact that David was born in the Year of the Rooster on the Vietnamese zodiac. Huy Fong Foods is a family business, staffed by eight members of the family. The company has never advertised its products, relying instead on word of mouth.

Dikembe Mutombo

ILLUSTRATED BY DION MBD

Dikembe Mutombo Mpolondo Mukamba Jean-Jacques Wamutombo was born in Leopoldville (today Kinshasa) and is a member of the Luba ethnic group from the Democratic Republic of the Congo. Dikembe grew up dreaming of becoming a doctor. He moved to the United States in 1987 at age twenty-one to attend Georgetown University on an academic scholarship and soon was recruited to play basketball by legendary Georgetown coach John Thompson. After college, Dikembe was signed by the Denver Nuggets as the fourth overall pick of the 1991 NBA draft, which launched his impressive career as a center. Dikembe is commonly regarded as one of the greatest shot blockers and defensive players of all time. He won the NBA Defensive Player of the Year Award four times; was an eight-time All-Star; and was inducted into the Basketball Hall of Fame. All the while, Dikembe continued his studies and learned nine languages. He is also celebrated for the countless humanitarian efforts he has led in the Democratic Republic of the Congo.

Edwidge Danticat

ILLUSTRATED BY TRACY GUITEAU

Edwidge Danticat is an award-winning author, born in 1969 in Port-au-Prince, Haiti. When she was four years old, Edwidge and her younger brother were left in the care of her uncle and his wife when her parents moved to the US. At twelve years old, Edwidge and her brother were reunited with their parents in New York. Edwidge struggled to fit in, but found refuge in the library and in writing. She attended Barnard College, where she earned her BA in French literature and translation, before pursuing an MFA in creative writing at Brown University in 1991. While at Barnard, Edwidge wrote stories that became part of her first story collection, *Krik? Krak!* — a 1995 National Book Award Finalist. Her novel *Breath, Eyes, Memory*, was a 1998 Oprah's Book Club selection. In 2007, her book *Brother, I'm Dying* was a National Book Award Finalist and the winner of the National Book Critics Circle Award for Autobiography. She is also the author of several children's books, including *Untwine*, *Behind the Mountains*, and *Eight Days: A Story of Haiti*. She is world-renowned for her exploration of the experiences of the Haitian diaspora.

Ilhan Omar

ILLUSTRATED BY FAHMIDA AZIM

Ilhan Omar fled the civil war in Somalia with her family in 1991 and spent four years in a refugee camp in Kenya, before arriving in the US with her six brothers and sisters under a resettlement program. In 2016, she was elected to the Minnesota House of Representatives as a member of the Minnesota Democratic-Farmer-Labor Party, making her the first Somali American legislator elected to office in the United States. On November 6, 2018, Ilhan became the first Somali American elected to the United States House of Representatives, representing Minnesota's Fifth Congressional District. Along with Rashida Tlaib, she was one of the first Muslim women elected to Congress. Omar is also the first Muslim former refugee to be elected to the House and the first woman of color to serve as a US representative from Minnesota.

Jim Lee

ILLUSTRATED BY VANESSA FLORES

Jim was born in Seoul, South Korea, and grew up in St. Louis, Missouri. When at first he struggled to learn English, Jim felt like an outsider and found he could easily relate to the language of comic books. This is how his love of comics was born. In 1987, he became an artist for Marvel Comics. He penciled and co-wrote *The Uncanny X-Men. X-Men No. 1* in 1991, a spin off series, became the bestselling comic book of all time. In 1992, Jim helped found Image Comics, a creator-owned company whereby his studio, WildStorm Productions, created its own content. In 1998, Lee sold WildStorm to DC Comics and came on to run it as an imprint at DC. In 2010, Jim Lee became the new Co-Publisher of DC Comics. He has received multiple awards in recognition for his work.

Juana Gutiérrez

ILLUSTRATED BY JOSE RAMIREZ

Juana Beatríz Gutiérrez is a political activist and community organizer. She was born in 1932 in Zacatecas, Mexico, and moved to the United States in 1954. The mother of nine children and a lifelong resident of East Los Angeles, Juana began her activism by starting a Neighborhood Watch and developing sports booster programs throughout Boyle Heights. In 1984, she founded Madres del Este Los Angeles Santa Isabel (MELASI) when she and other mothers formed an opposition to a proposed prison project near their home. Juana later led MELASI to defeat two proposed toxic waste incinerators, a dump site, a chemical treatment plant, and an oil pipeline in the vicinity of hundreds of thousands of residents. MELASI has provided scholarship funds of over $300,000 to local students, established a water conservation program, developed a community garden, and addressed crime, unemployment, dangerous working conditions, and pesticide-filled foods. Juana's environmental and community work has inspired many people around the world.

Yo-Yo Ma

ILLUSTRATED BY GABY D'ALESSANDRO

Yo-Yo Ma was born in Paris, France, and spent his schooling years in New York City. He was a child prodigy, performing from the age of four. He graduated from the Juilliard School and Harvard University and has enjoyed a prolific career as both a soloist performing with orchestras around the world and a recording artist. He has recorded more than ninety albums and received eighteen Grammy Awards. In addition to recordings of the standard classical repertoire, he has recorded a wide variety of folk music such as American bluegrass music, traditional Chinese melodies, Argentinian tangos, and Brazilian music. His musical projects are infused with the idea that music brings people together.

Undocupoets

ILLUSTRATED BY YAS IMAMURA

In 2015, Marcelo Hernandez Castillo, Javier Zamora, and Christopher Soto founded the Undocupoets, a campaign to protest the discriminatory behavior of many poetry publishing contests that didn't let undocumented poets apply. The Undocupoets published an open petition asking ten renowned contests to revise their application requirements, and they succeeded in effecting change for more inclusive publishing. Following the petition, Janine Joseph and Esther Lin joined the campaigners to form an organization. The Undocupoets mobilize to promote the work of undocumented poets and raise consciousness about the barriers they face in the literary community. The Undocupoets Fellowship, in partnership with the Sibling Rivalry Press Foundation, is awarded to an undocumented writer annually.

Contributor Bios

ALINA CHAU is an award-winning filmmaker and artist. Her credits include the Emmy Award–winning *Star Wars: The Clone Wars* animated series, and numerous bestselling games. She illustrated *The Nian Monster*, which received the 2018 APALA Picture Book Honor. Having grown up in Hong Kong in an Indonesian Chinese family during the British colonial era and then immigrating to America, her unique cultural heritage strongly influences her artistic and storytelling voice. Her lyrical watercolors are highly sought after for art exhibitions worldwide and have garnered her a devoted fan base and the accolades of her peers. She lives in Los Angeles with her little Maltipoo, Piglet. Visit her at alinachau.com.

AIDA SALAZAR is the author of the middle grade novels *The Moon Within* (International Latino Book Award Winner), *Land of the Cranes* (Charlotte Huck Award Honor), and *A Seed in the Sun*; and the forthcoming picture book *Jovita Wore Pants: The Story of a Revolutionary Fighter*. She is a founding member of Las Musas, a Latinx kidlit debut author collective. She lives with her family of artists in a teal house in Oakland, California. Visit her at aidasalazar.com.

BIANCA DIAZ is a Mexican American artist and educator from Chicago's Pilsen neighborhood. Bianca believes that healthy communities can help people become happy, independent human beings who hold the power to help others. Using art and education as her tools, she strives to be instrumental in the collaborative creation of these communities. Visit her at biancadiaz.com.

DION MBD's full name is Dionisius Mehaga Bangun Djayasaputra, and he is an Indonesian illustrator/designer who lives and works between Brooklyn and Bandung. Dion received his Illustration BFA from Ringling College of Art and Design in Florida, where he grew his fascination with clouds. In his downtime, Dion is either cooking, listening to John Mayer, or cloud watching. Visit him at dionmbd.com.

FAHMIDA AZIM is an illustrator and storyteller. Her work explores themes of identity, culture, and autonomy. She's occasionally spotted in the *New York Times*, NPR, *The Intercept*, and *Vice*. Her debut book, *Muslim Women Are Everything*, is a groundbreaking collection of illustrated stories celebrating real and extraordinary Muslim women — one of the first of its kind. She's based in Seattle, Washington. Visit her at fahmida-azim.com.

GABY D'ALESSANDRO is a Dominican illustrator based in Brooklyn. She attended Altos de Chavón in the Dominican Republic and moved to New York to complete her degree in illustration at Parsons School of Design. Her work has appeared in many publications and projects for clients such as the *New York Times*, NPR, the Library of Congress, *National Geographic*, the Botanical Garden of Padua, and New York City's MTA. Visit her at gabydalessandro.com.

JOSE RAMIREZ is a Chicano artist who makes children's books, murals, and commissions for organizations, communities, and individuals. Ramirez is also an educator who has taught in the Los Angeles Unified School District for over twenty-three years and is currently teaching third grade. He received a BFA and MFA in art from UC Berkeley, and a California Teaching Credential from CSULA. His work has been exhibited nationally, including at the Mexican Cultural Institute in Washington, DC. He is the illustrator of the Pura Belpré Award–winning picture book *When Angels Sing: The Story of Rock Legend Carlos Santana*, written by Michael Mahin. Jose is the proud father of three daughters: Tonantzin, Luna, and Sol. Visit him at ramirezart.com.

KEN DALEY is an artist and an award-winning illustrator of *Joseph's Big Ride* and *Auntie Luce's Talking Paintings* (Kirkus Review Best Picture Book and Américas Award Honorable Mention). Ken draws inspiration for his work from his African Caribbean roots, his life experiences, and the people and cultures he encounters along the way. Ken was born in Cambridge, Ontario, Canada, and lives with his wife and two pets in Rhode Island. Visit him at kendaleyart.com.

NICOLE XU is a Chinese Canadian illustrator living in Brooklyn. She has worked on multiple editorial projects for the *New York Times*, NPR, *The New Yorker*, etc. and published her debut picture book, *All of a Sudden and Forever*, written by Chris Barton. Visit her at nicole-xu.com.

PAULO D. CAMPOS is an illustrator who grew up in Minas Gerais, Brazil, and throughout the United States as well. He originally went to school at the University of Connecticut and studied management information systems, but during his senior year he came to the realization that he needed to pursue his passion. Paulo promptly dropped out and applied to the School of Visual Arts. He was accepted, and four years later, he now has a BFA in Illustration. It has definitely been the best decision he has made so far! Visit him at pdcampos.com.

RAHELE JOMEPOUR BELL is a picture book maker and a picture book lover. She feels very much like the character of Alice in this new wonderland of America. As an immigrant, Rahele has learned to celebrate something in her everyday life, even something as simple as the sun on her brown skin or letting her hair fly in the breeze while remembering her roots in Persia. Visit her at rahelestudio.com.

TRACY GUITEAU is a Haitian American artist who found her purpose at an early age, and headed for Providence, Rhode Island, to get a degree in fashion design at the renowned Rhode Island School of Design. She loves putting hours into her craft and her dreams with a positive sense of exuberance. Her art is exhibited all over the world, and she was handpicked by LeBron James's digital media company and former No. 1 world tennis player Naomi Osaka to do an art collaboration for the Coachella Valley Music and Arts Festival. Visit her at tracyguiteau.com.

VANESSA FLORES is an illustrator and storyteller raised on plátanos and old-school salsa. After years of working as a graphic artist at Scholastic Book Fairs, she left to pursue a career in children's book illustration. She is the illustrator of the middle grade book *Eat Bugs: Project Startup.* She loves being an active part of the art and Latinx community in Orlando, Florida, by participating in art shows and pop-ups. She is a member of the Society of Children's Book Writers and Illustrators and the Orlando Giant Illustrator collective. Visit her at vanessafloresart.com.

YAS IMAMURA is an illustrator from Portland, Oregon. She's done product design for companies like Anthropologie, Papyrus, and Sanrio, and has her own greeting card shop called Quill & Fox. She's also illustrated children's books for publishers like Innovation Press, HarperCollins, Penguin Books, Albert Whitman, Houghton Mifflin Harcourt, Little Tiger Press, Magic Cat, Nosy Crow, Sleeping Bear Press, and others. Visit her at yasimamura.com.

Anthologist Note

I am an immigrant. I moved to the United States to pursue my dream of becoming an animator. I applied to the UCLA Film School because there was no graduate-level animation study in Hong Kong at the time. Eventually, I established a successful career and also found my chosen family. America became my home.

I was sworn in as a naturalized US citizen on July 23, 2018. Given the contemporary racial and ethnic politics, and the fight for equality and social justice for people of color and immigrants, I felt the need to contribute to this country that I call home. This became the genesis of this book.

I want to celebrate the triumph and stories of people of color, who are often underrepresented. Some of these stories are well-known, while others are unknown. Telling both of these types of stories is vital. They represent the ordinary people who are invaluable to the communities, yet often underappreciated.

I wish to show that the true beauty of the American Dream is not wealth or fame. It's possibility. The American Dream is a beacon of hope. At its best, American society, culture, and history are a beautiful, complex tapestry woven by generations of brave souls who crossed oceans and borders for many reasons, but all of them seeking a chance at something better. Many immigrants came with few possessions, but a wealth of optimism and hope, and immigrants shaped and continue to shape America's fabric and the meaning of what it is to be American.

The book's decorative elements are inspired by traditional decorative art from various cultures, such as the Japanese cherry blossom, the Chinese symbol of blessing, and the East India peacock. These images symbolize the cultural richness that immigrants of color have added to America's beautiful tapestry!

— ALINA CHAU

Author Note

It is a great privilege to have been asked to join Alina's incredible project — to write poems of people who, like me, came to the United States from other countries.

History books will tell us we are a country of immigrants. But the truth is that our country was stolen from Native Americans by European settlers and built by enslaved people as well as by immigrants. A truer statement would be: We are a nation of the robbed, of the enslaved, and of immigrants.

We titled the book *In the Spirit of a Dream* in direct reference to the idea of the American Dream — the notion that you can achieve anything you wish if and when you live in "the land of opportunity," the United States. Many immigrants come clinging to this dream with an aspiration for freedom, for prosperity, for safety, to live a better life than they previously experienced. However, the dream does not come true for many immigrants, especially those who come from countries not in Europe. Often, the journey to get to the United States is fraught with dangers and difficulties and it is no dream at all.

Past administrations have used fear and hate-filled stories about immigrants of color to pass unjust laws and create systems to keep us from successfully migrating into the United States. The purpose of this book is to show how immigrants, from across the globe, use the belief in their dream to challenge, to innovate, and to excel despite these circumstances. There are so many stories to tell. Some are known and some are unknown, and immigrants don't need to be exceptional to be valued. The stories featured in this book are a testament not so much to the American Dream but to the resilience of the human spirit to rise above adversity and to thrive. I hope they inspire you as much as they do me.

— AIDA SALAZAR

The text for this book is set in 13 point Plantagenet Cherokee Regular. Designed by Ross Mills in 2000, this expansion of the Plantagenet font contains Cherokee characters. It is one of the earliest modernist typefaces that incorporates the ideology of the Bauhaus movement in Germany.

The display font is set in Loyola Pro Extra Bold. This font was designed by Rodrigo Araya Salas and Franco Jonas, and published by Rodrigo Typo. It is a sans serif font specifically designed for titles.

The wraparound cover illustration was created by Alina Chau.

The book was printed on 157gsm FSC Golden Sun Matte paper and bound at RR Donnelley Asia.

The production was overseen by Jael Fogle.

The manufacturing was supervised by Shannon Rice.

The book was designed by Marijka Kostiw and edited by Kait Feldmann.